W9-DCM-005

Portrait of
WASHINGTON D.C.

 Portrait of America Series

Portrait of
WASHINGTON D.C.

Photography by Robert Reynolds
Text by James Cary and Thomas K. Worcester

■■ **GRAPHIC ARTS CENTER PUBLISHING COMPANY**
■■ *Portland, Oregon*

Cover: The Statue of Freedom towers over The United States Capitol dome. Erected in 1863 the figure stands more than 287 feet above Jenkins Hill.

Title Page: Sculpted by Thomas Crawford, the Statue of Freedom is 19½ feet tall and weighs 7½ tons. The 13 fluted columns surmounting the cap represent the 13 original colonies.

Acknowledgements: Welcome to Washington, D.C., by James Cary reprinted by permission from *Western's World,* the magazine of Western Airlines. Published by Frank M. Hiteshew and Associates; copyright 1979.

International Standard Book Number 0-912856-55-6
Library of Congress catalog number 79-55979
Copyright © 1980 by Graphic Arts Center Publishing Company
2000 N.W. Wilson Street, Portland, Oregon 97209
Typesetting: Paul O. Giesey/Adcrafters
Printing: Graphic Arts Center
Binding: Lincoln and Allen
Printed in the United States of America.

Right: Visitors walk amidst the ring of flags beneath the great national memorial to George Washington. Begun in 1833, this obelisk, 555 feet 5⅛ inches tall, was opened to the public 55 years later in 1888.

The fresco Apotheosis of Washington by Constantino Brumidi, which glorifies
the work of George Washington, was painted on the concave surface of the
interior of the Capitol dome. Brumidi, then 60, finished the masterpiece in 1865,
taking almost one year to complete it.

The great white dome of the United States Capitol is a major symbol of the nation. St. Peter's Church in Rome provided the model for this dome, which was constructed during the early 1860s. It replaced a smaller one.

Between the Capitol and the Washington Monument, the Mall stretches for one and four-tenths miles. Visible are the Smithsonian "castle" on the left and the National Museum of Natural History on the right.

"We have built no national temples but the capitol, we consult no common oracle but the constitution."

Rufus Choate, *member of Congress*

Inside the National Archives Building, the original copy of the Constitution of the United States is on display, preserved in a helium-sealed case, which is hydraulically lowered into a bomb and fire-proof vault each night. Above it are the Declaration of Independence and the Bill of Rights.

The Library of Congress is a great national storehouse of knowledge and, although not a lending library, its facilities are open to the public as well as to Congress.

The great colonnade of the Lincoln Memorial dwarfs an early morning jogger. Each of its 36 Doric columns represents a state of the Union during Lincoln's administration.

The Executive Office Building, situated next door to the White House, originally housed the State, War, and Navy departments. When this massive, rococo structure was built during 1871-1887, it was considered the world's largest office building.

The New Executive Office Building viewed from the Jackson Place entrance attests to the increasing staff that supports the office of the President. The building is an excellent example of contemporary architecture fitting comfortably among the old.

The White House, completed in 1800, reconstructed after the British burned it in 1814, first renovated in 1902, and then again in 1948-1952, has retained its simplicity, beauty, and dignity. President Theodore Roosevelt officially changed the name from the President's House to the White House.

The Jackson statue by Clark Mills is made from the bronze of cannons captured by Jackson in the War of 1812. It stands in LaFayette Square where it was placed in 1855.

Flanking the Capitol are the House Office Buildings in the foreground and the Senate Office Buildings at the upper right, all of which were purposely designed as subdued structures surrounding the Capitol.

Welcome to Washington D.C.

by James Cary

ORIENTATION

They tower against the sky, white and symbolic, the shaft of the Washington Monument and the massive dome of the Capitol —and appropriately so. For they are the first sentinels of the nation's governing city to be sighted by the visitor descending from the sky or approaching by land, and they make excellent reference points.

In the 1.4-mile span between them, or in separate enclaves nearby, lies the heartland of the great attractions and power centers that make Washington, D.C., a city of magnificent sights and sounds, of continuous spectacle and unfolding history, of parks and museums, a city impossible to devour quickly but subject to highly rewarding, continuous sampling.

Because the fare offered is sumptuous and vast, there is a problem of where to begin, where to end, and what to leave out in between, in partaking of this movable feast. But the Capitol is one highly recommended starting place. There, beneath the dome's soaring arches, the House and Senate enact the laws of the nation from Monday through Friday noon when, as if by some mysterious alchemy, the lawmakers begin disappearing for the weekend.

A visit to the office of your senator or congressman will provide a pass permitting you to watch either chamber in session. Or if you are venturesome you can always find some members congregated at midday at a favorite nearby watering hole, the Monacle Restaurant, one block from the Capitol, for lunch. Even more, however, will be at their desks gobbling down a sandwich, or grabbing a hasty meal at the restaurants in the Capitol provided for House and Senate.

At night it is a different story. Some make what they hope will be career-building appearances on the cocktail circuit in the swank, bedroom suburb of Georgetown, where some of the nation's premier hosts entertain. This provides an opportunity for new members of Congress to be seen, sometimes heard, and hopefully to raise the level of public awareness of their presence. Still others congregate at one of Washington's excellent, and very expensive, French

restaurants —San Souci, Le Bagatelle, Dominique or Rive Gauche —mulling legislative problems and tomorrow's strategy on the House or Senate floor. But as many as possible will make it home to grasp a few hours out of the public view and away from their high-exposure jobs.

Aside from the members, however, the Capitol itself has a story to tell that is readily available on one of the regularly scheduled public tours. There are excellent paintings, including a famous rendition of the signing of the Declaration of Independence, in the Capitol rotunda. Statuary Hall is peopled with giant figures of the past; and if you can talk your way into it, you may also get a glimpse of the crypt in the Capitol basement where it was originally intended that George Washington be buried.

The building itself goes back to September 18, 1793, when the cornerstone of the North wing was laid as part of the overall city plan drawn up by Pierre Charles L'Enfant, a French artist and engineer who followed the Marquis de LaFayette to America. Before 1790 the area now occupied by the capital city was partly marshland. There were some manor houses and plantations, but it was sparsely inhabited except for the nearby communities of Alexandria, laid out in 1749, and Georgetown, a thriving, shallow-water tobacco port on the Potomac River. In 1790 Congress finally selected a 10-square-mile site near the river, purchased it for $66.66 an acre, and called in L'Enfant to tell them where and how to begin erecting the buildings needed to house a functioning government. The total government bureaucracy numbered 126 clerks when the move from Philadelphia was finally made in June, 1800.

Standing on the Capitol steps now, looking west out over this vastly changed city, you are adjacent to some of the nation's finest museums, lining both sides of the long, grassy, tree-bordered Mall fronting on the Capitol. On the right are the National Gallery of Art, housed in two buildings, the Museum of Natural History and the Museum of History and Technology. You can spend days in each and see only part of the exhibits. On the left are the very popular Air and Space Museum, a tourist must, the Smithsonian Institution, the Hershhorn Museum and Sculpture Garden and the Freer Art Gallery. And at the end of that sward, no matter which side you traverse, is the Washington Monument, rearing 555 feet high, encircled by flags snapping in the breeze. A Park Service kiosk there can provide you with information and tickets to board any of the blue-and-white tourmobiles that visit most of the city's major attractions.

But if you prefer to strike out on your own, what lies nearby is pure gold. From the Monument grounds you can look north, across a circular park called the Ellipse, to the south grounds of the White House, with its rolling hummocks placed there by Thomas Jefferson, a towering elm planted by John Quincy Adams and, up close to the executive mansion, magnolia trees brought from his Tennessee home, the Hermitage, and planted there by President Andrew Jackson. The Jackson magnolias are now gnarled and aged, but they have yielded young slips that have been returned to the Hermitage to replace the parent stock there after it died, thus preserving the strain.

When a state visitor is in town the south grounds become a scene of pageantry. Cannon boom on the Ellipse—19 guns for a prime minister, 21 for a head of state. A five-service honor guard is aligned splendidly across the grass and official welcoming remarks are piped out over loudspeakers. Often what is said there becomes tomorrow's headlines, foreshadowing major events to come.

THE WHITE HOUSE

Like the Capitol, the White House is a living, functioning museum, embracing history past, present and future. It is also the home and office of the President. Within its confines he confers daily with top advisers, meets and negotiates with foreign officials, and tries to persuade members of Congress to accept his views on needed legislation. The executive mansion is open to the public Tuesday through Saturday, 10 A.M. till noon. Just pick up a free ticket at the booth on the Ellipse immediately south of the White House. Guides will direct you to the east entrance.

You pass first through the East Wing, catching a glimpse enroute of the library, to the Vermeil Room and Diplomatic Reception Room, where the late President Franklin D. Roosevelt used to deliver his Fireside Chats. A turn to the right and you ascend the stairs to the State Floor and visit the Green, Blue and Red Rooms, the State Dining Room and the East

Room. Under the giant crystal chandelier in that magnificent chamber the bodies of Presidents Abraham Lincoln, William McKinley and John F. Kennedy lay in state. It was also in this chamber, at that time unfinished, that Abigail Adams, the first First Lady to live in the White House, hung her wash.

The White House was a different place in those days: cold, drafty and damp. Nevertheless President John Adams, who moved in during November, 1800, wrote his wife before she arrived: "I pray heaven to bestow the best of blessings on this house and all that shall hereafter inhabit it. May none but honest and wise men ever rule under this roof." Those words are now carved on the marble mantel in the State Dining Room.

His appeal for the best of blessings was soon to be sorely tested. On August 24, 1814, British soldiers, retaliating against the destruction of public buildings by U.S. troops in Canada during the War of 1812, captured Washington and burned both the President's House, as it was then called, and the Capitol. Both were rebuilt and back in use again by 1819. Improvements were to follow soon. Spring water was first piped into the White House in 1834, gas lighting followed in 1848 and hot water heating in 1853. The first elevator came in 1881 and, during the administration of Benjamin Harrison, it was wired for electricity. A modern electrical kitchen was not installed, however, until 1930. But by 1948 it was apparent the building was deteriorating rapidly and had become dangerous to live in. It creaked and groaned at night, even swayed and shifted at times. An architectural examination determined some of the old wooden beams had weakened. They were inadequately supported, the heavy ceilings had dropped several inches, and the foundations were too weak to support the walls.

President Harry Truman moved to the nation's official guest mansion, the historic Blair-Lee House across Pennsylvania Avenue from the White House, while the entire structure was renovated. The old sandstone walls, still showing smoke stains from the British torching, were retained, but this time were provided with concrete foundations. The wooden beams and brick supporting walls were replaced by a modern steel framework. In March, 1952, the Presidential family returned to the residence.

In your passage through the White House, you will see many mementoes of this past, of its presidents and their families. And if you are fortunate the First Lady may wander down to visit for a few moments with those in the long line of guests. Your chance of seeing her, or some other member of the First Family, will be even further enhanced if you plan your visit far enough in advance to request a VIP tour pass from your congressman or one of your two senators. Each has a small allocation of these and they are in great demand, but if obtainable are worthwhile. The VIP tours begin earlier than the public tours and are usually in small groups led by a personal guide to explain the exhibits as you proceed.

All this public activity in the White House does not extend to the second and third floors where the President has his living quarters, or to the West Wing where he conducts most of the nation's business from his Oval Office.

NOTEWORTHY PLACES

So much for history. As you exit from the White House under the North Portico and move down the driveway to the Northeast Gate, you will be in position to view some of the flamboyant displays of floral beauty for which Washington is noted, both on the north lawn, in LaFayette Park across the street and elsewhere in the city. In the spring the capital is awash with tulips, daffodils, multihued azaleas and flowering trees, including the famous cherry blossoms from Japan rimming the nearby Tidal Basin and on the Monument grounds. Later these give way to geraniums, roses and other summer flowers. It was largely through the efforts of former First Lady, Lady Bird Johnson that Washington truly became a city of flowers.

Such displays make a leisurely stroll south down 14th Street, past Washington Monument, extra rewarding. A short distance beyond Independence Avenue you will come to the clearly marked visitor's entrance to the Bureau of Printing and Engraving. Turn right. You will emerge on a catwalk above the working level where the nation's paper money is printed, examined, sometimes rejected for flaws, stacked and bundled, ready for distribution to the nation's banks. Within a few minutes you will see more money than you are apt to see ever again in one place for the remainder of your life. It moves by at an annual rate of $20 billion. The Bureau also designs and prints Treasury bonds, bills, notes, certificates of indebtedness, postage, customs and revenue stamps, food coupons and even White House invitations. But 99 percent of its time is taken up with producing currency in $1, $2, $5, $10, $20, $50 and $100 denominations. In this instance that old cornpone joke very definitely applies: they do not give free samples. Indeed the security is very tight for workers and visitors alike.

Immediately east of the Bureau lies one of Wash-

ington's most scenic areas. The long water channel of the Reflecting Pool picks up and mirrors the image of the Washington Monument, and leads to the stately Lincoln Memorial. There the brooding, seated figure of Lincoln, with the great cadenced words of his Gettysburg Address engraved on the marble walls behind him, is one of the most moving sights in Washington. It was from the Memorial's steps that the Rev. Martin Luther King delivered his "I Have a Dream" address on August 28, 1963, during a massive rally supporting full rights for blacks; while less than a mile away the statue of Thomas Jefferson, ensconced in his own white marble memorial pavilion on the south bank of the Tidal Basin, overlooked the scene. The author of America's Declaration of Independence was symbolically watching another American seeking access to the full privileges of United States citizenship.

At the Lincoln Memorial you are only a short automobile or bus ride from Arlington Cemetery, where you can stand on the front steps of the old Custis-Lee Mansion, called Arlington House, the former home of Robert E. Lee, and gaze out over the city. To your immediate front are the graves of the martyred President John F. Kennedy and his brother, Sen. Robert F. Kennedy. And off to your right, the Tomb of the Unknown Soldier. There a sentry paces 24 hours a day before a Tomb enshrining the remains of three servicemen "Known But to God," from World War I, World War II and the Korean conflict.

The site is deeply rooted in American history. The land was originally purchased by John Parke Custis, son of George Washington's wife Martha by a first marriage. Two of John Parke Custis' four children were later adopted by Washington and one of them, George Washington Parke Custis, had a daughter who married Lt. Robert E. Lee, later to lead the Confederate Army of Northern Virginia during the War between the States. The estate was taken over by Union forces during that conflict and later converted into a national cemetery.

A few miles to the south, astride a rise overlooking the Potomac River, is the magnificently restored Washington home, Mount Vernon. It is a story in itself and well worth a leisurely visit. Perhaps more so than most old Southern mansions it conveys the life of the 18th-century country squire, with its smokehouse and separate buildings for cooking, washing and carrying on of the many handicrafts practiced in that day.

The central section of the Georgian home was built in 1743 by George's half brother, Lawrence, who later willed it to the nation's first President. Washington added the wings and columned portico. He yearned to live there but was absent most of the time — from 1775 to 1783 leading the Continental Army during the Revolution, again in 1787 when he presided at the Constitutional Convention, and finally from 1789 to 1797 when he was President. He died two years later. He and Martha are buried in a brick mausoleum just down the slope from the mansion. After his death the house fell into disrepair but was eventually acquired by the Mount Vernon Ladies' Association of the Union and fully restored. It stands now, resplendently white in the afternoon sun, on the banks of the Potomac.

That river flows endlessly past so much of what was and is the past and future of the nation. It skirts the Pentagon, focus of U.S. defense efforts. It touches Roosevelt Island, where a heroic statue of Teddy glowers aggressively over a sylvan scene. It reaches north and east to such historic sites as Harper's Ferry, where John Brown was to run to ground after an unsuccessful anti-slavery uprising in October, 1859; and much further south it flows by the historic old city of Alexandria, known so well to Washington and the leaders of his day. Washington's pew in Christ Church there is still preserved. This lovely old English country-style building, constructed of native brick and stone between 1767 and 1773, is open to the public.

Also nearby is Woodlawn Plantation, a gift from Washington that was the home of Nellie Custis, Martha Washington's granddaughter, and her husband. Within Alexandria are the Old Presbyterian Meeting House, built in 1774, Lee's boyhood home,

and Gadsby's Tavern, made up of two buildings and erected in 1770 and 1792. The Fairfax Resolves, forerunner of the Bill of Rights, were prepared there. Washington also danced with Martha in the second-floor ballroom.

While there is much in today's Alexandria that Washington could recognize, he would have more difficulty in the city of Washington itself. It is a bustling crossroads of the world where leaders of all nations come to confer with American government officials. The facade is constantly changing. Hundreds of new office buildings have been erected in the last decade. A modern subway system moves rapidly beneath its streets. Suburbs have spread across the countryside in every direction. Property values have soared. More and more of the nation's top corporations have transferred their headquarters here to be close to the seat of power.

Along with this growth has come a flourishing cultural life. The Kennedy Center, with its magnificent tier of three theaters, graces the banks of the Potomac. Ford's Theater, where President Lincoln was shot, has been fully restored and offers a full fare of dramatic productions, as well as a fine, attached museum. Across the street, the small residence where Lincoln was taken after he was fatally wounded, has been converted into a museum. And up and down Pennsylvania Avenue, the avenue of the Presidents who traverse its broad sweep from Capitol to White House during every inauguration, a major restoration project is underway to make it truly a national concourse of great and stately beauty.

A Permanent Site for the Federal Government

By Thomas K. Worcester

JENKINS HILL

Jenkins Hill rises to an elevation of about 88 feet above the Potomac River about two miles from the confluence of the Anacostia River and the Potomac in western Maryland. Two hundred years ago, the hill was covered with lush underbrush and woods, and in the immediate surroundings only an occasional rustic home interrupted the virgin nature of the area. Nearby were the cities of Georgetown, Maryland, and Alexandria, Virginia — the centers of commerce and social life in that section of the lower Potomac.

Jenkins Hill today is the site of one of the most significant buildings in the world: the United States Capitol. How it came to be placed there is a story of the remarkable genius of the early men who determined the nature of this country. How it remains is a continuing tribute to those founders and to other gallant men and women who have nutured the idea that is America.

The hill and its near environs (including Alexandria and Georgetown) are part of a 100-square-mile tract of land selected by President George Washington as the site of a Federal City, the seat of government for the nation. The city was born of compromise, and has lived in contrast and paradox throughout its history.

Perhaps the idea of a Federal City became serious because of an incident in 1783. Continental Army troops seeking back pay marched on Philadelphia where Congress was in session. The members of Congress, fearing harm from the aggrieved soldiers, called on the Philadelphia militia for protection, but the militia refused to act. The aroused soldiers soon encircled the Pennsylvania State House where Congress met, and, with bayonets fixed, demanded their overdue pay. But Congress dismissed the demand. James Madison, alarmed for the safety of the lawmakers, called for an immediate adjournment of Congress, and suggested it was "time to remove to some other place." But Congress remained in session until the usual hour of closure, then recessed for the

weekend. On the following Tuesday, Congress retreated to the safety of Princeton, leaving the Philadelphia hall to the soldiers. But the idea of a separate federal territory with a militia to protect the Congress was afloat and members now talked seriously of a location.

The question of a permanent site for the federal government had been raised in Congress as early as 1779. At that time, it seemed likely that the government would be located in some existing city, where there would be ready-made facilities for the legislators and the federal workers. But what city? More than one had been suggested as the ideal location for the government: there was Boston, where the first shot of the Revolutionary War had been fired; and Yorktown, where victory was grasped; and Philadelphia, where independence had been proclaimed. New York, Newport, Williamsburg, Wilmington, Lancaster, Trenton, Annapolis—all sought the honor.

Debate on the location of the national capital lasted until 1790, when the issue appeared hopelessly deadlocked in a North-South standoff. But through the careful political engineering of Thomas Jefferson and Alexander Hamilton, a compromise was reached: in trade for having the national capital situated on the Potomac River, southern Congressmen would support a bill which shifted fiscal responsibility for the state war debts to the federal government. This measure was of particular benefit to the northern states which had had the major share of financing the Revolutionary War. Thus the northern states received needed funds, while the southern states rejoiced at having the capital site nearby. Congress took two further steps in 1790 to settle the establishment of the Federal City: Philadelphia was selected to be the temporary site for ten years, or until the first Monday in December, 1800, when the capital would be moved to its permanent site; and secondly, President Washington was entrusted with choosing "on the river Potomac" a territory, ten miles square, which was to become the federal territory and the permanent seat of the United States Government.

What would be the nature of the Federal City? A residential city for legislators, statesmen, and federal employees? Or a center of commerce for trade with the world's ports? Or a mixture of both? And what of its future?

President Washington had little trouble deciding on the location for he was familiar with the area of the Potomac, having ridden through its forests and over the hills much of his life. He chose the spot where the city now stands for its intrinsic beauty, its location relative to the Potomac, and for its centrality.

Congress also authorized the president to appoint three commissioners to survey the district, under his direction, and to establish title to the land in the name of the federal government. The state of Maryland ceded about 68 square miles to the government and the state of Virginia 32 square miles, thus establishing the federal district. From the very beginning a confusion of names was inherent in the district and the city, for the cities of Georgetown and Alexandria were already in existence, but were included in the new federal district. But the three commissioners appointed by President Washington named the new Federal City "City of Washington," and the area in the state of Maryland, outside the City of Washington and Georgetown, was called the County of Washington. The area in Virginia outside Alexandria was known as the County of Alexandria. Thus in its initial stages, the District of Columbia, so named by the commissioners, included the City of Washington, Georgetown, Alexandria, the County of Alexandria (Virginia) and the County of Washington (Maryland).

For the design of the new Federal City, George Washington selected Major Pierre Charles L'Enfant, a French engineer who had served with the American forces during the Revolutionary War. When he learned of the plans for the new city, L'Enfant wrote to President Washington from New York:

"Sir: The late determination of Congress to lay the foundation of a city which is to become the capital of this vast empire offers so great an occasion of acquiring reputation to whoever may be appointed to conduct the execution of the business that your Excellency will not be surprised that my ambition and the desire I have of becoming a useful citizen should lead me to wish a share in the undertaking.

"No nation, perhaps, had ever before the opportunity offered them of deliberately deciding on the spot where the capital city should be fixed...And, although the means now within the power of the country are not such as to pursue the design to any great extent, it will obvious that the plan should be drawn on such a scale as to leave room for the aggrandizement and embellishment which the increase of the wealth of the nation will permit it to pursue at any period, however remote. Viewing the matter in this light, I am fully sensible of the extent of the undertaking."

L'Enfant has been described as proud, haughty, intractable, and with an "untoward" temper, but he also was honest, loyal, and extremely gifted. Washington perceived him as a scientific man with considerable taste and professional knowledge, "better qualified than anyone who has come within my knowledge in this country." The President informed L'Enfant to begin work at once.

L'Enfant left New York and went to Georgetown in early March, 1791, where he found the selected site clouded by mist and soaked by heavy rainfall. Eager to begin, L'Enfant rode horseback throughout the area, and though visibility was restricted, he was enthralled by the countryside and the prospects it offered for the city. In his first survey of the area he selected Jenkins Hill as the site of the Capitol, or Federal House as the designer called it. He later wrote:

"I could discover no one (spot) so advantageously to greet the congressional building as is that on the west end of Jenkins heights, which stands as a pedestal waiting for a monument."

L'Enfant's vision of the Federal City was that of an area where the government officials and federal employees would work in the surroundings of monuments and memorials to the famous. His plan called for avenues up to 160 feet wide, frequent circles and squares, diagonal avenues that cut across the city to allow traffic to move from one area to another with ease, and a grand avenue from the "Federal House" to the "President's Palace."

L'Enfant's plan has been said to resemble a wheel, with the Capitol at the hub. The plan is original, though in some ways its major features—open vistas, major arterials from point to point—are similar to the Versailles, where he spent his early years. The broad avenues and circles also were used in Paris, another city with which he was intimately familiar.

The vigor with which L'Enfant pursued the plan eventually led to his dismissal as supervisor of construction of the city. This was after he ordered the destruction of a house belonging to the cousin of one of the District Commissioners, which was being constructed contrary to L'Enfant's plans.

In his later years, Pierre Charles L'Enfant roamed the streets of Washington and haunted the halls of the Capitol, vigorously defending his plan for the Federal City. He died in 1825, and he was buried at the foot of a tree on the Digges property near Washington. His entire estate at that time was valued at $46.00.

The credibility of his plan has captured the imaginations of city planners decades later, though even the brilliant L'Enfant could not envision the congestion that modern automobile traffic would cause in his beloved city.

While some steps were taken to institute the L'Enfant plan during the early years of the capital's life, for the most part Washington remained a backward town, with dirt streets, poor sanitation facilities, and undeveloped land until the 1870's. Then, through a series of circumstances that can only be considered fortuitous to the development of the city, a man was elevated into power in the city who launched Washington on the course that has made it the city it is today. That man was Alexander Robey Shepherd.

In 1871, Congress established a territorial form of govenment for the District of Columbia, with a governor, an 11-member legislative assembly, and a 22-man house of delegates. President Grant appointed Henry D. Cooke as governor of the district, and Alexander Shepherd was made a chairman of the Board of Public Works. Shepherd, a native of Washington, was an ex-member of the city council and head of a Citizen's Reform Association. He soon became the most powerful man in the territorial government, and with the energy and ambition of a zealot set out to make the city the most beautiful in the world.

Shepherd constructed many miles of sewers, paved the streets, put in sidewalks, moved railroad tracks, established parks, and installed street lights. He also planted trees—hundreds of trees. By 1873 he was made governor of the District, and had nearly total control of the operations of the District. But a financial panic that year, coupled with a Congressional investigation which unearthed a heavy debt for the city, forced Congress to abolish the territorial form of government, and Shepherd's brief reign over the city was over. Not, however, before he had made the improvements give credence to the original plan of L'Enfant. Though castigated at the time, Shepherd proved to be a geniune saviour for the city, and since has been honored as the "Maker of Washington."

L'Enfant's plan withstood the test of scrutiny and comparison once again 100 years later when Congress established a commission to plan for the entire District of Columbia what L'Enfant had done for the Federal City area. Charles Moore, chairman of the National Commission of the Arts, wrote in 1929:

"After two years of study, in light of the finest examples the world has produced, this commission reinstated the authority of the L'Enfant plan and carried it to its logical conclusion in new territory. The action reflected credit not only on the genius of L'Enfant, but also on the commission itself which had the wisdom to recognize the extreme merit of the original plan and the sense — and modesty — to build upon it." *

In 1909, a grateful Washington paid tribute to Pierre Charles L'Enfant in a way that had not been done in his lifetime. His remains were disinterred from their obscure burial place and brought to Jenkins Hill, where he lay in state in the rotunda of the Capitol, an honor reserved for the nation's highest acclaim. He was then reburied in Arlington National Cemetery, high on the hillside overlooking his Federal City. Marking the grave is a granite slab on which is incised a copy of L'Enfant's original conception, a plan which the designer once said "must leave to posterity a grand idea of the patriotic interest which promoted it."

**L'Enfant and Washington*, 1929, Johns Hopkins University Press.

THE DISTRICT OF COLUMBIA

To most Americans, political Washington brings to mind the President and the Congress, as well it should, because the executive and legislative branches of the government wield an authority that is unique to the city and the District.

The city and the District — are they different? Not really, at least not in terms of political subdivision. Washington and the District are one and the same and the government of the city is, in fact, the government of the District of Columbia. And the District of Columbia is a political subdivision unlike any other in the United States. At the same time, it is a combination of *all* other political subdivisions.

Confusing? Yes. Martin K. Schaller, former executive secretary for the District of Columbia explains the relationship this way:

"The District of Columbia is a state, a county, and a city all in one, and the mayor exercises many of the functions of a governor, county executive, and mayor. We have almost all the governmental functions that you would find in a state, a county, and a city. For instance, there is no other city in the United States that has a department of motor vehicles. That is always a state function. No city government has a department of insurance. That also is a state function. Boards of education operate on city, county, and state levels, so our superintendent of education would be a commissioner of education in a state government. We are in competition with all the states for federal grants, and

this is one of the 'governor' functions that the mayor exercises. We have a district income tax that is analogous with a state tax, and a D.C. real estate tax, a personal property tax, and other minor taxes —motor vehicle, tobacco, alcohol, business inventory, business franchise, and so on."

Some of the confusion about the political subdivision of the region has existed since the establishment of the District of Columbia. The original District was made up of approximately 68 square miles of the State of Maryland and 32 square miles of the State of Virginia. Included within those boundaries were five separate political entities: the existing cities of Georgetown (Maryland) and Alexandria (Virginia); the new Federal City being planned by Pierre L'Enfant; the county of Washington, which was all the area outside of Georgetown and the City of-Washington in the State of Maryland; and the County of Alexandria, that area outside of the City of Alexandria in Virginia. In 1846, Congress returned the 32 square miles of land in Virginia to that state, reducing the size of the District of Columbia to the 68 square miles in the boundaries of Maryland, and comprising three political subdivisions: Georgetown, the City of Washington, and the County of Washington. In 1895, Congress merged Georgetown with the City of Washington, ending the former's status as a separate city.

Since its inception, the District of Columbia has had various types of government. From 1800 to 1871, commissioners or mayor-city council types of government existed. But in 1871, Congress made a historical change when it declared the District a legal territory, just like other territories before they became states, with a governor, a two-chamber territorial legislature, and a delegate to the U.S. House of Representatives. Even then the District was not self-governing: the governor was appointed, as was one house in the legislature. The other house was elected by citizens of the District. But Congress ended the territorial period in 1875 when it felt the governor was exercising too much authority, and put in its place an appointed board of commissioners.

In 1967, Congress established a mayor-city council form of government in the District of Columbia. Residents of the District still did not vote for their officials, for the mayor and the nine-man council were appointed by the President and confirmed by the Senate.

In May 1974, "home rule" was granted to the residents of the District of Columbia. Now citizens elect their District officials, have broadened legislative power, and a role in local planning.

Washington would not be self-sufficient without federal revenues. The city has no large industries. The business of government is the main business in the city, and provides the primary source of revenue. The second biggest business is tourism — about 19,000,000 tourists visit Washington each year.

Some 290,000 federal employees work in the area, and another 44,000 are city or District employees. The primary sources of revenue for the District is the income tax, sales tax and property tax.

"There is the national flag. He must be cold, indeed, who can look upon its folds rippling in the breeze without pride of country."

Charles Sumner

Old Glory's broad stripes and bright stars wave in a breeze. Congress enacted a resolution in 1777 making the flag of the United States 13 stripes alternating red and white with 13 white stars in a field of blue. In 1818 the body ammended it to specify a white star for each state.

The Octagon House, completed in 1801, contains excellent examples of Federal period architecture. The oval staircase elegantly descends three floors with a continuous handrail. It is one of the few structures to survive the British burning of Washington in 1814.

The Treaty Room is located on the second floor of the Octagon House, where in February 1815 the treaty of Ghent was ratified, ending the War of 1812. This house was President Madison's residence for about nine months after the White House was burned. In the rooms on the second floor Madison carried out his duties as President.

Guarded 24 hours a day, the Tomb of the Unknown Soldier in Arlington
National Cemetery enshrines the remains of three unknown servicemen from
World War I, World War II, and the Korean conflict. They symbolize those
who gave their lives for America in war.

Tombstones of America's war dead line the quiet, rolling hillsides of Arlington National Cemetery in Virginia. It was first used as a cemetery in 1864 during the Civil War. President John F. Kennedy's grave with its eternal flame is also located here.

Approximately 600 Japanese cherry trees line the shores of the Tidal Basin and usually bloom in April each year. Blossoms are pink upon opening, then turn snow white, lasting for about 10 days.

"No man is good enough, no group of men, to be trusted with unrestrained powers."

Thomas Jefferson

The statue of Jefferson by sculptor Rudulph Evans towers behind two visitors casually resting against one of the 26 white marble columns of the Thomas Jefferson Memorial. Located on the south shore of Tidal Basin, the memorial was dedicated in 1943.

An ornate lamp post embellishes the walk and driveways on the east Capitol grounds. The lamp post was erected approximately 100 years ago, before most of the city's landscaping took place.

The stone bust of *Aysh-Ke-Bah-Ke-Ko-Zhay (Flat Mouth), a Chippewa Chief, is located on the third floor in the senate wing of the Capitol. The Chippewa, or Ojibwa, Indians were one of the largest tribes in America.*

The Washington Cathedral towers above the summit of Mount Saint Albans in northwest Washington. It is one of the great cathedrals built in modern times, adhering closely to medieval architecture.

The control tower at Dulles International Airport in nearby Virginia monitors the arrivals and departures of dozens of planes each day. Eero Saarinen designed this innovative airport facility which serves the Washington metropolitan area.

The White House, oldest public structure in Washington, has been the home of every president except George Washington. The North Portico, added by Jefferson, gives the structure a distinct southern colonial quality.

"May none but honest and wise men ever rule under this roof."

John Adams

The familiar picture of George Washington by Gilbert Stuart hangs in the East Room of the White House. It is one of three objects that has been in the house since it was first occupied.

This statue is one of two large statues on the east end of the Arlington Memorial
Bridge. They were a gift from the people of Italy to the people of the United
States.

Townhouses in historic Georgetown, now a district of homes, shops, and restaurants, was a thriving community when Pierre Charles L'Enfant arrived in 1791 to lay out a federal city on the adjacent woodland.

The National Museum of Natural History, an integral part of the Smithsonian
complex, has a collection of more than 50,000,000 bird and animal specimens,
for exhibit and for scientific study.

The Fenykovi elephant, a 12-ton African giant and the largest species of
land animal of modern times, is a popular exhibit in the National Museum of
Natural History.

Henry Bacon designed the Lincoln Memorial, located in Potomac Park, to resemble a Greek temple. It was dedicated in 1922 and is one of the most popular visitor sites in the capital.

"Here was a man to hold against the world, a man to match the mountains and the sea."

Edwin Markham of Lincoln

A visitor gazes at Lincoln, seated 19 feet above the pedestal inside the Lincoln Memorial. The sculpture, created by Daniel Chester French, was carved from 28 blocks of Georgia marble.

The Freer Gallery of Art, containing approximately 10,000 catalogued items, houses one of the world's most distinguished collections of oriental art. This is the interior of the Chinese art room.

A marble statue of General Ulysses S. Grant by Franklin Simons stands in the rotunda of the Capitol, a gift from the Grand Army of the Republic—an organization established by Civil War veterans.

A statue of Marquis de LaFayette looks out across LaFayette Square located directly across Pennsylvania Avenue from the White House. A lifelong friend of George Washington, the Frenchman aided colonists and fought in the Revolutionary War at Washington's side.

The Supreme Court Building, constructed of Vermont marble, was begun in
1932 on the east side of the Capitol. Established by Article III of the Constitution,
the highest court of the United States heard its first case in 1789.

The National Air and Space Museum covers the entire spectrum of aerospace history and contains more than 60 aircraft and numerous spacecraft and rockets. The lunar module is the twin to that used in 1969 for man's first landing on the moon.

"I look forward to an America which will not be afraid of grace and beauty."

John F. Kennedy

An eighteenth century bust of Louis XIV, a gift from the Kress collection, is displayed in the National Gallery of Art. The gallery maintains a collection of paintings, sculpture, and graphic arts dating back to the twelfth century.

The Bartholdi Fountain stands south of Independence Avenue from the Botanic Gardens. These gardens were originally built to house botanical collections of nineteenth century expeditions.

A gift from the People's Republic of China in 1972, Hsing Hsing, the famous
giant panda, together with his mate, Ling-Ling reside in the National Zoological
Park. Exchanged with the Peking Zoo for two musk-oxen, the giant pandas live
in air-conditioned quarters because their natural habitat is cooler than normal
temperatures in Washington.

Standing in front of the south entrance of the Treasury Building is the statue
of Alexander Hamilton, first Secretary of the Treasury. Hamilton possessed one
of the greatest financial and organizational minds in the young republic.

Ducks paddle leisurely down the old Chesapeake and Ohio Canal near Lock 20. During the 1870s, the 185-mile canal along the north bank of the Potomac River was full of traffic carrying coal from the Cumberland mines in Maryland.

The Marine Corps War Memorial recalls the dramatic raising of the colors on Iwo Jima after a costly battle in 1945. Situated north of Arlington National Cemetery, it honors the men of the U.S. Marine Corps who gave their lives for their country since the corps was formed in 1775.

NATIONAL GUARD
MEMORIAL

*The late afternoon sun throws the shadow of an eagle clutching arrows
across the face of the National Guard Memorial on Massachusetts Avenue.
Placed under the jurisdiction of the states in peacetime, the National Guard
can become a part of the armed forces in war.*

A bronze lion adjoining the front entrance of the Corcoran Gallery of Art keeps out a wary eye for all visitors. William Wilson Corcoran, a wealthy local banker, founded the gallery in 1870, which now contains collections of paintings, sculpture, and ceramics.

The East Building of the National Gallery of Art, designed by I. M. Pei, opened in 1978. An Alexander Calder mobile hangs in the marble-lined, glass-roofed central court where exhibits are displayed.

Not only Americans, but foreign visitors and members of diplomatic services from all over the world, come to Washington to work and visit. After the government, tourism contributes the next largest amount of dollars to the district.

Focused on modern art, the collections and exhibits of the Hirschhorn Museum
are housed in a cylindrical structure designed by Gordon Bunshaft.
This excellent collection of modern painting and sculpture was donated by
Joseph H. Hirshhorn, and is a part of the Smithsonian complex.

The grand foyer of the John F. Kennedy Center for the Performing Arts overlooks the Potomac River. The seven-foot-high bronze bust of President Kennedy on the south wall is the dominating element of the 630-foot-long hall. On the right are three large modern auditoriums which simultaneously accommodate concerts, ballet, opera, plays, and symphonies.

"I am certain that after the dust of centuries has passed over our cities, we too, will be remembered not for victories or defeats in battle or in politics, but for our contribution to the human spirit."

John F. Kennedy

The Albert Einstein Memorial, located on Constitution Avenue in front of the National Academy of Sciences, was created by sculptor Robert Berks. The seated bronze figure is three times life size.

At day's end, commuters wend their way home over the Arlington Memorial Bridge. Along the far shore is Lady Bird Johnson Park on Columbia Island and on the hill above is the Custis-Lee Mansion National Memorial, former home of Robert E. Lee.

With flared nostril, this horse is one of the 14-foot high statues outside the
Federal Trade Commission Building, a W.P.A. project commissioned in 1938.
The government created the F.T.C. in 1914 to check the growth of monopolies
and to preserve competition.

George Washington's mansion at Mount Vernon as seen from the main gate. The central structure was built in 1743 by Lawrence, Washington's half-brother, and the last additions were completed in 1787 by George Washington after he inherited the estate.

A tasteful brick wall divides the stable yard from the kitchen garden. Using Washington's detailed notes, The Mount Vernon Ladies Association of the Union has restored and operated Mount Vernon since 1860.

Neighborhood children frolic on the equestrian statue of General George Washington in Washington Circle. In 1775 Washington was named commander-in-chief of the Continental forces.

Sunlight sparkles across the Reflecting Pool and backlights the 50 flags circling the Washington Monument. Also visible from this vantage point at the Lincoln Memorial are the Smithsonian on the right and the Capitol at the far end of the Mall, with the Library of Congress behind and to its right.

*A congressional act established the Smithsonian Institution in 1846 when
James Smithson, an English gentleman, left his endowment to create "an establishment for the increase and diffusion of knowledge among men."*

This dress, worn by Dolly Madison at a reception in the White House in 1816, is only one object in the enormous collection of precious treasures the Smithsonian has amassed.

A white swan greets the early morning beside the tranquil waters of the Reflecting Pool. As the architect of the new federal site, L'Enfant's plan was to create open spaces for vistas and major arterials with broad avenues and circles.

The Shrine of the Immaculate Conception is an impressive building on the campus of Catholic University in northeast Washington. The university is one of Washington's many institutions of higher learning which include Georgetown University, George Washington University and American University.

The Library of Congress, built in 1879, has an impressive interior of carved marble, accented with mosaics, statues, and archways. Among its priceless treasures are the Gutenberg Bible and the Gettysburg address recorded in the hand of Lincoln.

"—There is, in fact, no subject to which a member of congress may not have occasion to refer."

Thomas Jefferson

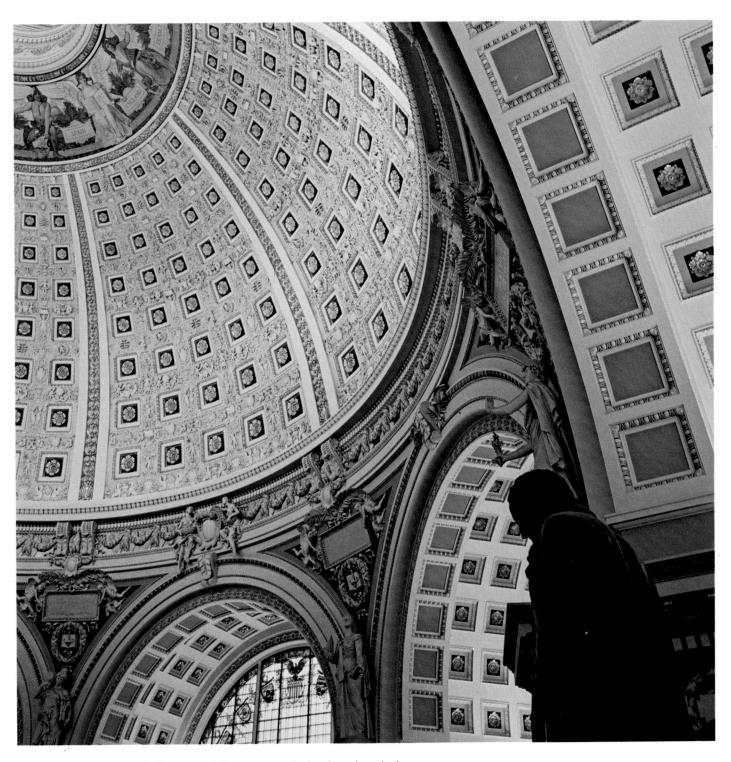

Established in 1800, the Library of Congress serves the legislative branch of government but is open to the public as a reference library. Today it is one of the world's great libraries containing more than 75,000,000 items.

A sea nymph triumphantly bestriding an infuriated sea horse is part of the fanciful fountain by Hinton Perry located in front of the Library of Congress on First Street.

Spirited horses draw a cannon across a small part of the 252-foot-long memorial to General Ulysses S. Grant, commander-in-chief of the Union Army during the Civil War. Henry Shrady spent 19 years working on the memorial, completed in 1922.

Built in a modified Pantheon form, the Thomas Jefferson Memorial is a circular structure with a dome ceiling. Prominently located on the Tidal Basin, this setting befits the importance of Jefferson in the nation's history.

The massive Ionic columns of the Thomas Jefferson Memorial catch the last rays of sun. Across the Tidal Basin, the Washington Monument, over half a mile away, dominates the horizon—a reference point throughout the capital.

Located nine miles upriver from the capital, the Potomac River abruptly descends nearly 80 feet over Great Falls as the river leaves the Piedmont. In 1754 George Washington suggested a canal to skirt these falls.

Theodore Roosevelt Island, located due west of the John F. Kennedy Center in the Potomac River, is an 88-acre wilderness preserve authorized by Congress in 1932 to honor President Roosevelt's contributions to conservation. The bronze and marble monument of Roosevelt is located on the island.

"—and that government of the people, by the people, for the people, shall not perish from the earth."

Abraham Lincoln

The colors are lowered at the Custis-Lee Mansion National Memorial in Arlington National Cemetery. Beyond lies the nation's Capitol, where Congress held its first session in 1800, and the Washington Monument.